VICTOR D'AMICO # EXPERIMENTS IN CREATIVE ART TEACHING

A Progress Report on the Department of Education,

1937 – 1960. The Museum of Modern Art, New York.

Distributed by Doubleday & Company, Inc., Garden City, New York.

All photographs unless otherwise credited are by Soichi Sunami

Published by The Museum of Modern Art, 1960
11 West 53 Street, New York

Second printing, 1963

Library of Congress Catalog Card Number: 60 – 7938

Typography and design by Susan Draper

Printed in England by W. S. Cowell Ltd., Butter Market, Ipswich

ACKNOWLEDGMENTS

I wish to thank all the teachers of the People's Art Center who over the twenty-two years have carried on the various experiments and projects with distinction, and the children and adults without whose cooperation this program could not have taken place. I want in particular to express my gratitude to Jane Bland, Jean d'Autilia, Zoltan Hecht, Lois Lord, Moreen Maser—master teachers all—who helped to build the philosophy contained in this book and who put it into practice. Many thanks go to Charles Cook, Robert Iglehart, Arthur Young—founders of the National Committee on Art Education—and to Edith Mitchell and Olive Riley for their significant contributions to the Committee and to art education in general. Great credit is due to Dorothy Knowles, Elizabeth Fuller, and Elinor Weis for their skill and devotion in helping to administer the complex program of the Department of Education.

VICTOR D'AMICO

TABLE OF CONTENTS

PREFACE

While this volume is a report on the growth and activities of the Museum of Modern Art's Department of Education during the twenty-two years of its existence, it is fundamentally an exposition of its underlying ideas, methods, and explorations. The Department did not begin full-fledged, but as an experimental project with a gallery of exhibitions for children and young people of high school age, and with a circulating program of exhibits for only ten schools. The project grew as it attempted to find solutions to problems in art education involving the child, the adult, and the art teacher. New directions were explored as new needs arose, such as establishing an art center for war veterans or experimenting with television as a means for teaching art. The educational philosophy presented here is not merely theory: it is a result of practical experience over an extended period of time. We hope that the ideas and methods described will be of service to other educators and museums in extending or developing their programs, and that they will provide encouragement and a resource for the art teacher as he carries on his important work of developing creative individuals.

photo Len Ross

PART I

The Department of
Education and Creative
Teaching

THE ROLE OF THE DEPARTMENT OF EDUCATION IN THE MUSEUM

For over twenty years the Department of Education of the Museum of Modern Art has been a pioneer in serving the art needs of children, young people, adults, and schools. Throughout the country, educators seeking fresh ideas and improved methods of teaching look to the Museum for help and leadership. While the Museum is in a broad sense an educational institution, with all its departments contributing, the Department of Education has the specific responsibility of dealing directly with the development of the individual and of cooperating with teachers and schools. Parents in the New York City area who discover that art instruction in the schools is either below standard or non-existent, or who wish additional art opportunities for their children, find the solution in the classes of the People's Art Center. Adults who desire to pursue art as an avocation or as an absorbing activity for their years of retirement find a variety of opportunities offered.

The Department of Education, as an integral part of the Museum, has at its disposal the rich reserves of all Museum departments, for various purposes from designing a publication to working out the content of courses and exhibitions. The People's Art Center adjoins the Museum and gives its students immediate access to the finest collection of modern art in the world as well as a wide variety of current exhibitions in every phase of contemporary art.

The Department of Education has complete freedom to establish its philosophy and to explore new ideas and methods of educational advancement. It is not in any way subject to indoctrinary influences or to vested interests which seek to exploit the individual child or adult.

IS CREATIVE EDUCATION AN ESTABLISHED FACT?

Contrary to common belief, there is no one sound and assured method of art education recognized and established in all schools and communities in the country. What is termed "creative education" runs the gamut from the most indoctrinary to the most laissez-faire teaching. Creative education is actually in a period of transition and confusion. At no time since the introduction of the idea of self-expression has there been greater danger of decline in aesthetic standards and a return to reactionary methods. For example, many accept the mere physical requirements, such as paints and collage and construction materials, as sufficient for creative experience, while at the same time there is a growing insistence on technical skills and aids for their own sake, such as drawing, perspective, and color wheels.

IMPORTANCE OF THE ART TEACHER AND OF SOUND TEACHING METHODS

While an individual may at times achieve high creative standards on his own, most children and adults need the guidance of experienced and sensitive teachers. A grave misconception resulting from the self-expression era is the notion that children are self-taught. Even when certain children do create automatically, they cannot as a rule sustain this creativeness over an extended period without skilled guidance. The art teacher is vital to the education of the individual: his selection and preparation are, therefore, of greatest importance.

We are often asked on what basis we choose teachers for the People's Art Center. Staff members range from those with no degrees to some with masters' degrees and a few working toward doctorates; they include practicing painters and sculptors as well as craftsmen in ceramics and jewelry. There is no simple definition of the qualifications of a good teacher, although there are perhaps some basic common denominators. Not only must the teacher be experienced in the area in which he is expected to guide others, it is necessary for him to be adequately aware of concepts of psychological growth, both creative and general, of the particular age level or levels of his students. It is a sad commentary that teachers colleges provide either a great deal of aesthetic preparation with little in psychology or too much psychology with superficial training in the arts. Unless a teacher has a balanced and integrated knowledge of both, he cannot be adequate. The Center also seeks in its teachers a warm human attitude, an inspired feeling toward the arts, a respect for individuality, and a devotion to excellence of design and craftsmanship. Either through training or preference, some teachers are better suited to teach one particular age level than another—the young child, the adolescent, or the adult. Some can teach two or more age levels; but this does not make them better teachers. Effectiveness depends on an ability to stimulate and develop the creative interests of others and to communicate the aesthetic values that underlie all creative achievement.

BASIC AIMS OF CREATIVE TEACHING

The main objective of the Department of Education is to develop the most effective philosophy and method of teaching art and to promote their wide application. While approximately 1200 children and adults are taught each term in the classes of the People's Art Center, its ideas and methods have reached millions of children and teachers in a program that has attained world recognition and influence through publications, television, and the Children's Carnival.

THE FUNDAMENTALS OF ART

The principal aim of the teaching is to develop each individual's sensitivity to the fundamentals of art and thus to increase his creative power and his awareness of the vast heritage of contemporary art and that of the past. What is meant by "fundamentals"? Not, as most people believe, such criteria as skill or good draughtsmanship, technical knowledge of color harmonies and rules of perspective, or factual data on the history of art. These are not fundamentals but, at best, only means to a particular expression or achievement. They are incidental to actual fundamentals more vital and dynamic: development of individuality and sensitivity to aesthetic values in works of art, in human relations, and in one's environment. Jane

photo Arline Strong

Top: *Collage*, by Robert, $5\frac{1}{4}$ years
Bottom: *Men Rowing a Boat*, by John, $5\frac{3}{4}$ years

Bland, instructor on the staff of the People's Art Center, states in her recent book, *Art of the Young Child:* "Giving a child opportunity and time to explore and encouraging him to do so is fundamental. . . . It is fundamental to provide young children with the opportunity and encouragement to express freely. . . . Acceptance and respect of what the child creates is fundamental. . . . It is fundamental to learn techniques as they are needed. . . ."*

The matter of recognizing or explaining these attitudes presents a difficult problem at times. Parents often insist, for example, that their children should learn to draw more accurately, and students in the adult classes are easily attracted by clever techniques instead of sensitive expression. Developing true and lasting satisfaction is a more profound matter than giving what they think they want. Often it means opposing superficial wishes to reach a deeper need or desire.

* New York, The Museum of Modern Art, 1957, pp. 33ff.

10

photo Len Ross

NEED FOR EDUCATING THE PUBLIC

It is extremely important to enlighten the public, namely the parent, family, school, and community, so that the need for good art education will be recognized. Many parents do not give their children opportunities in art unless they feel their children are talented; and many schools, especially at the elementary level, fail to provide art or art teachers because they do not regard art as an essential subject. As a result, the museum art center, in our case the People's Art Center, often provides the only sound art education available. Even this teaching may be undone by a parent who insists on stereotypes or a grade teacher who uses obsolete methods.

Mere permissiveness is not a solution to the problem. The parent must not only be willing to have the child take art; he should understand the basic aims and methods of art education so that he can be a continuing constructive influence at home. The administrator, school principal, or superintendent who is merely in favor of having art in the curriculum, but who has no further understanding of its personal or cultural value, may destroy the value of the art experience by selecting an indoctrinary teacher, by endorsing contests, or by giving awards on the basis of superior skill and performance.

Art education depends on the will and understanding of the parents, administrators, and school boards who dominate the curriculum, and who together can provide any possible kind of art education. A basic concept of the new education established over thirty years ago was to give every child a well-balanced education with art indispensable to that balance.

photo Arline Strong

photo Len Ross

QUESTIONS OFTEN ASKED BY PARENTS

The questions parents ask reveal their frequent misunderstanding of the importance of art for children. Following are questions most often asked, collected over a period of time by the staff of the People's Art Center.

1. *Does my child have talent?*

There is no reliable means of determining the presence or amount of talent in children. Several experiments and studies are being made but none considered adequate by most educators. General criteria are so broad that they are impractical for determining specific ability. While talent in children may exist, the method of evaluating it must necessarily be personal and subjective. Even when and if an adequate measuring stick is devised (and one device will not do for all age levels) the major problem will be deciding what conclusions to make and what action to take as a result of this knowledge. One cannot assume that the child at six or eight is destined for an art career, because experience shows that strong interests or abilities change in later years. The problem is at least a complicated one.

2. *Should my child take art if he has no talent?*

There is no correlation in children between having talent and deriving satisfaction from the art experience. It has been established that art is necessary to the emotional and cultural growth of all children. A talented child might benefit more by having art than would the average child, but since talent in children cannot yet be determined the matter is open to question.

3. *Why don't you teach children the fundamentals?*

As has been suggested, this question often erroneously implies that perspective rules or value scales are fundamentals. Better educators regard them only as secondary techniques and skills. Today we consider the fundamentals to be the development of individuality and the awareness and sensitivity to aesthetic values in works of art and in the natural environment.

4. Why don't you teach my child perspective?

Perspective is being taught today, but not by the academic methods of the past. Parents who ask this question often recall that in their youth they learned perspective rules as isolated exercises; they often admit it was a boring and a fruitless experience. Perspective is a technique for representing the illusion of reality, one of many ways of indicating space. The young child uses art expressively and emotionally; perspective would confuse his expression and hamper his direct, simple, and personal quality. He often expresses his knowledge of space by other means. As he grows older and is curious about perspective, it becomes part of his learning, but he is taught only those elements which he can comprehend or which he needs for his expression. He may, for example, wish to represent the converging lines of a table or want to know how to make an object seem to lie flat on it; but this is no reason for forcing the entire science of perspective on him at this time. It has been found that techniques and skills learned in isolation become mechanical and meaningless. Only when integrated with expression do they have power and meaning for the child.

5. When are you going to start teaching something?

A parent may feel that when his child can recite a rule or point to what he has been taught there is more proof of learning than when he cannot; but these are superficial evidences of learning compared to the more vital ones of growing satisfaction, greater independence, or sensitive expression. If a parent begins to recognize and evaluate these deeper values, he will be a greater asset to his child. Unfortunately, in many instances parents wish to project their own obsolete training of a generation ago on the dynamic creative teaching of today.

6. Isn't my child going to do something different next term?

Learning is a continuous process: it often involves continuation of the same concepts, techniques and subject matter, year after year. As the child matures, these concepts become deeper and more complex in their challenge and study. For example, while the child always uses color as part of his expression, at the age of 3 or 4 he experiments to discover how colors behave and how to invent his own, whereas at 13 or 14 he may study the use of color as an expression of mood or feeling or how color values affect harmonies. Difference or change in itself is no criterion. Faced with the tendency in modern living to effect changes, to get many things easily, by turning the dial from one TV station to another or by acquiring a large number of toys, the emphasis on concentration, with penetration into a problem, is desirable. The major difference we seek from term to term is a change of attitude, an increasingly profound feeling about the world, achieved through greater mastery of art concepts—not merely a superficial change of activity or material.

7. When should you begin to correct the child's mistakes?

Parents who ask this question are usually under some misconception. They may be looking at the child's art from a conservative adult standpoint and insisting on exact representation and realistic effect; and they may regard as mistakes all expressions which do not conform with their preconception. They may see as mere ineptitude, tolerable while the child is still very young, his imaginative use of color, his exaggeration or distortion of form for the purpose of emphasis, his use of personal symbols for a man, an animal or a house; but they look forward to the day when he will outgrow this stage and paint more recognizable objects. The child's natural way is to use art as a personal language; with exaggeration and distortion, he invents ways of telling us about his ideas, impressions and feelings. This natural approach results in the exciting designs which make children's art so vital and which artists admire. Without imagination or personal invention, not only children's art but all art would be sterile and dull. Children, of course, do make mistakes, but their errors are incidental to the art expression, diminishing as they gain power and experience.

A Jungle, by Otis, 8½ years

Tree in Snow, by Ann, 8 years

8. *Should the child learn to draw before he can create?*

This is a rather persistent question asked about children of all ages. The assumption is that the child should master the skill to represent the appearance of objects before he attempts to compose pictures or express his feelings and ideas in paint, clay or other media. It would be as reasonable to insist that children amass a wide vocabulary and learn the rules of grammar before they are allowed to speak. But drawing skills were used in teaching art over forty years ago. From plates prepared for them, children in the elementary grades were made to copy vases, tables, houses, and such natural objects as plants and trees; in high school they drew from stuffed birds and still life; in art school they copied plaster casts or drew from the human figure. The result was that drawing became a mechanical operation. When the student was finally permitted to express his own ideas, his perception had become so atrophied it was difficult or impossible for him to do so. In the broadest sense, drawing is expression or depiction of an observed or imagined form. Drawings can be executed in a variety of ways and in a variety of media.

Children must draw as an integral part of their expression, regardless of the apparent result, just as they stumble in learning to walk or misuse words as they learn to talk.

9. *What is wrong with copying?*

When a child copies another person's drawing or painting, he is merely reproducing the result without having had the experience that brought it about. It would be a little like copying a poem or an arithmetic problem: he would not have learned to use words or rhythm to express an idea or to follow through a mathematical process. Not only would the effort and labor be wasted, but the child might be deceived into believing that he had acquired the same status as the artist he imitates. In addition to being harmful to creative growth, copying is unethical because it is a form of counterfeiting or stealing.

The argument sometimes advanced in favor of copying is that the old masters copied and often had ateliers or workshops where apprentices copied them. Today this practice is challenged as a way of learning by many outstanding educators. If copying has any value, it can only

Indoctrinary teaching stifles creativeness.

be for the mature adult student who is able to analyze the process and follow its various stages. Copying can never be condoned as a valid way for teaching children.

10. *What is wrong with coloring books?*

The majority of the various coloring books on the market have a common fault: they have ready-made shapes for the child to color with crayons or watercolors; he must "keep inside the lines." Some books have a colored picture on one page, the same picture in outline for the child to color on the facing page. Sometimes there is no picture to copy from but simply outlines of animals or people, or just designs. The objection is that these books require a precision unnatural for the young child which leads to cramped execution and rigidity in concept. It is important to recognize that young children are by nature free and spontaneous in their expression and tend to work by automatic direction or kinesthetic feeling. Any activity which inhibits this natural tendency is harmful. The notion that working within outlines produces neatness and is therefore good discipline ignores a real value in the

interest of a superficial one. In addition, though many books have stylized pictures of poor quality, giving the child another person's drawing to fill in implies that he cannot draw well enough for himself; this undermines his confidence. Coloring books at their worst may therefore destroy natural creative expression, induce imitation, and injure the child's taste. A coloring book does not provide a good activity for the child: the parent or relative who offers one as a gift is really working against his own good intentions.

11. *Do you teach only modern art?*

This is, of course, a logical question to ask of a school which is a part of the Museum of Modern Art. The word "modern" is often applied only to abstract art and not to the vast range of expressions which actually comprise modern art. It would be as indoctrinary to teach all children to express themselves abstractly as it would to have them draw literally from objects. If education is to develop the child's personality, it must nourish every kind of expression. If a child tends to work abstractly, the teacher will try to develop that particular expression; if another child tends to work realistically, the teacher will guide him. But each child must work in a way natural to him. The real problem is to free the child of his clichés or imitated mannerisms and to help him discover his own way of seeing and expressing.

A PRACTICAL EXPERIMENT IN PARENT EDUCATION – *Classes for Parents and Children*

Among the most successful means of educating the parent are the Parent-Children Classes, where fathers and mothers paint, model in clay, make constructions, and engage in most of their children's activities. The aim of these classes is to give parents the shared experience of observing their children create under the guidance of a skilled art teacher. While other means of parent education have been practiced over the years, such as lectures on children's creative development, personal interviews between teacher and parent, observation of classes, and even workshops, none have proved so valuable as actually working alongside the child throughout an entire semester, watching him grow and growing with him.

The Museum's first Parent-Children class was organized in 1950. Over the years, they have increased steadily both in number and in interest. During the first years of the classes, parents were self-conscious and fearful of creating. Some were concerned that their achievements would not compare favorably with those of their children. These fears have practically disappeared as parents learned the value of the classes for their children. Many parents have even discovered a deep creative desire of their own and have subsequently joined an adult class in painting, sculpture, or crafts.

Each class for parents and children is limited to about a dozen members; the six children range from three to five years, an age level important in creative growth, as well as the period children and parents work best together. In the first session, for parents alone, the teacher discusses the aims of the class, points out what to look for in the child's behavior and work, and outlines the procedure to be followed. While each teacher proceeds somewhat differently, most prefer to have parents work independently. The children are placed at low tables, either directly in front of the parents' high tables or in a central group with the parents arranged as three sides of a square around them. In this way, the children, whose eye level is below the height of the parents' tables, are not inclined to be influenced by what the adults do.

As the sessions progress, the teacher first motivates or starts the children, and then gives her attention to starting the grown-ups. Throughout the class the parent is able to observe how the teacher behaves with the child in answering questions, making comments, or introducing new projects and materials. Sometimes parents work together with their children, trying out the same project or motivation; or they work side by side on different projects. But parents are advised not to do the work for the children nor to make suggestions which might inhibit the children's own ideas and efforts.

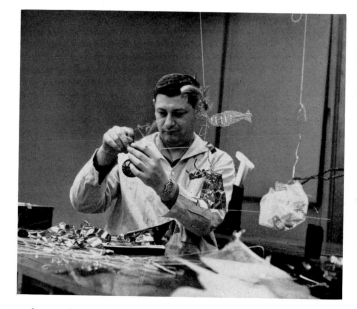

Father making mobile.
Photo Len Ross

Parents and children work at tables convenient to their size.

photo Impact, Frank Donato

Child discusses construction with her mother.

photo Arline Strong

The Museum is particularly interested in a number of problems in art education. Some of these have existed for many years, while others are just emerging due to changes in educational philosophy and to pressures on art from both inside and outside the schools. The outcome of all these problems, however, will vitally affect the status of art education today and its ultimate future.

CONTESTS AND COMPETITIONS –
The Child Always Loses

Contests and competitions for children in elementary and high schools are a persistent problem that have posed a threat to art education for many years. Awards range from a simple honorable mention in the form of a ribbon or certificate to the gift of art materials, scholarships to art schools, or sums of money. Some contests have worthy objectives, such as the promotion of safety or health, while others sponsored by commercial enterprises provide a selfish and economical means for advertising a product. Regardless of the aims or auspices, contests are detrimental to art education.

The Museum has opposed contests for years and has, both on its own and in cooperation with other institutions and art associations, tried to educate the public to recognize the dangers involved. Contests persist, however, for a number of reasons. They receive more attention than any other single art activity in the school. Many have financial backing from commercial enterprises and are given coverage in newspapers and magazines. Principals and administrators often favor them because of the prestige which winning may bring to their schools; parents are attracted by the attention it calls to their children and the glory reflected on themselves. Even some art teachers yield to contests because of the honor it brings their subject. In spite of these apparent advantages and the spot-lighting of a few individuals, all the children, even the prize winners, suffer as a result of the contest.

The argument is often advanced that children should learn to compete because life is competitive and contests provide a necessary discipline. Competition can be advantageous if it conforms with the aims of art education and if it contributes to values important to the child's growth and which he understands.

But contests produce a psychological problem because only a few can win while the majority are doomed to the frustration of failure. This is, of course, contrary to the broad objective of art as a necessary part of every child's general education. Because of the excitement of publicity and prizes and all the ballyhoo which attends contests, the normal satisfaction of creating is lowered. Even if only the potential winners take part, contests create an atmosphere in the school psychologically deterrent to education.

A contest has a disruptive effect on the continuity of teaching, breaking the rhythmic day by day process of normal growth. A succession of contests can destroy a whole teaching program. In one large city the art supervisor complained that the demands made on the schools by contests were so great as to make it almost impossible to maintain any continuity in teaching. Art teachers are constantly besieged from all sides to have their children participate in contests. Opposing these competitions calls for great diplomacy and fortitude.

A basic objection to contests is that they focus on the end product; art education is concerned with the process of creating and with values not clearly recognized in the finished product. Furthermore, contests are often judged by standards which are too sophisticated or on an adult level. Juries often include prominent artists or business men who admire mere technique or subject matter without understanding the creative expression of children. And different standards of varying juries confuse the child, who is unable to analyze these differences.

Even the winners of contests stand to lose in the long run. Because of the emphasis on the finished product, winners tend to repeat or imitate themselves in the hope they will win again. If they fail in successive attempts, they look upon their winning as the high point in their young careers, and at an early age regard themselves as "has beens." Contest promoters are disinclined to award prizes to the same children time after time even though they merit it. For both "democratic" and promotional reasons, the prizes tend to be spread to as great a number of children as possible. One New York City high school, for example, was disqualified from entering a national competition because it took most of the top honors year after year.

Contests, therefore, constitute a danger in art education since in the long run they benefit only the sponsors. The National Committee on Art Education, an organization of outstanding art educators sponsored by the Museum of Modern Art, in 1952 passed the following resolution as part of a longer statement of its policy against contests on the elementary and high school level. "The Committee on Art Education believes that it has become the professional responsibility of teachers of art to express their disapproval of sponsored contests and competitions in the general art program of the elementary, junior high, and high school. Where the art program forms a part of the general education of children, the introduction of contests and competitions promoted by commercial or community agencies is educationally unsound."

If parents and general educators who recognize the dangers to children would add their support toward eliminating contests from the schools, one great handicap to creative education would be removed.

THE GIFTED CHILD - *Emphasis on Specialization*

While a great deal of attention has been paid to the average or normal child, the gifted child has been overlooked or has been required to follow a slower pace. Interest has been focused on this problem recently in practically all areas of learning. Many of the gifted become indifferent to their subjects because of the lack of challenge and fail to achieve their potentiality. This is also true in art education where the "talented" student does not find the curriculum planned for the majority

sufficiently demanding to absorb his superior interest and ability.

The general trend is to set up special classes for gifted students and teach them under a more advanced curriculum. While this is an expedient solution, it raises new problems and questions, particularly in the arts. As we have mentioned, there are no valid tests for measuring talent in art, and any selection must, therefore, be made on an arbitrary basis or through a compromise with tests which are only partially successful and perhaps misleading. One danger in classifying a student as gifted in art is the sometimes resulting belief that he should make art his career. There are thousands of students majoring in art in the high schools of our country whose demonstrated ability indicates no possibility of their anticipated success in careers in fine or commercial art. The result is that these schools are preparing young people for a frustrated adulthood. Even if the objective is education for a richer cultural life, isolation in groups or classes sets up an elite which is abnormal both for the special students and for the entire school community; art loses its status as a universal human expression. With the removal of superior students, the class made up entirely of average children loses the challenge and leadership given by superior students. An environment of students with a wide range of abilities is more natural and is closer to the situation the superior student will find in life. This does not, however, solve the particular problem for the gifted.

The staff of the People's Art Center held several meetings on the problem of the gifted child in its own curriculum. It was pointed out that there are several grades of gifted children; for example, superior students average about one to a hundred, while the very superior may occur only one to a thousand. In most classes there is at least one student who stands out above the others. There would have to be several degrees of special classes if the principle of isolation or independent teaching were followed through. Any such plan was rejected unanimously by the faculty because it would sacrifice too many valuable objectives in the hope of achieving a dubious one.

The solution adopted for our purposes, and one applicable to many school situations, is to retain all students in their age level groups while stepping up the curriculum for a superior student by giving him more challenging projects at his own rate of learning. By developing the discipline of independent work, such students may select or be given special problems according to their needs and interests and can move beyond the group if need be; at the same time they contribute to the group as a whole, giving it the benefit of their exploration and more profound learning. The problem of the gifted child lies largely in a sin of omission: teaching was conceived and curricula planned without him in mind. A broader study of education and more foresight in future planning can overcome this problem.

MORE SCIENCE, LESS ART

The most recent problem confronting art education results from the emphasis on meeting our need for national safety. All over the country, schools are adding and stepping up courses in mathematics and science without considering the effect on the student's total education or on his ability to master these subjects. Perhaps, as one principal of an outstanding private school has said, we are on another educational bandwagon: professional educators tend to pick one aspect of education, dress it up, give it all the ballyhoo, and, when it becomes stale, abandon it for something fresh. Of course it is vital for education to produce scientists for the nation's defense program; but this need not be done by coercing children who lack aptitude for science nor by giving a one-sided education to those who have it.

The unfortunate aspect of this problem is that the extra time given to science is in many instances taken from the arts. In some schools, art has been dropped from the curriculum entirely, while in others only those who do not rate high academically or who have a low I.Q. are encouraged to elect it. Some schools are compelling students with high I.Q.s to take an all-academic program with no art, against the students' own wishes and without their parents' approval. In some high schools, students who wish art take "bootleg" courses. That is, they have art after school in special groups without the knowledge of the school administration. No records are kept and courses are carried on in secrecy. So keen is the desire for art in many of our youth!

In one of his early addresses citing the need for more scientists, President Eisenhower emphasized that we must not develop science at the expense of the humanities, that the best science education was one balanced with the humanities. Eminent scientists and scholars have underscored the President's view by cautioning educators not to destroy our cultural foundations through a hysterical rush toward an overweighted science program. If we lose our cultural freedom and sacrifice the richness of a broad program of learning, we shall unwittingly play into the hands of the enemy and fulfill his wishes by our own lack of wisdom and foresight.

photo Len Ross

Creative Philosophy and
Methods for Teaching
Children, Young People, and
Adults

The People's Art Center

PART II

Collage, by Babette, 8¼ years

The Museum of Modern Art has for over twenty years been searching consistently for the best ideas and methods of teaching art to individuals of all ages from pre-school through adult. In its People's Art Center, the aim has been to develop the artistic sensibilities of children, young people, and adults and to help them understand and enjoy the arts of our time. Each semester classes are attended once a week by nearly 800 children and young people and 500 adults. For a number of children the Center provides the sole experienced guidance in art, as many schools do not have trained art teachers. There are, for example, no art teachers in the 620 elementary schools of New York City. Only eleven art supervisors direct all the classroom teachers, many without art training, who instruct the approximately 500,000 students in these schools. The Center provides the only creative experience for some students at the high school level either because the art teaching is inadequate, or because art is not included in the curriculum because of academic college requirements.

The aim of the classes for children and young people is to develop the creative ability and the appreciative powers of each individual to the highest possible level. Children are accepted as early as three years of age up through eighteen, when they are regarded as young adults. They are grouped according to age, keeping the range as narrow as possible within each class, such as 3–4 years, 5–6 years, 10–12 years, and so on. Classifying by age level has proved to be the soundest way from both the psychological and practical points of view. Any attempt to divide students on the basis of ability results in the undesirable competition discussed earlier. Even though the classification is chronological, parents often request that their child be placed in an older class because of ability. Such requests are declined. Some museums group their students in broad age spans, such as 4–12 years or 8–16 years, believing that this produces greater stimulation and variety of experience. While it is true and this is an advantage, the benefits are greatly outweighed by the difficulties such grouping presents. For example, it becomes more difficult to deepen the individual experience, and the younger children are made to feel less mature by the presence of the older ones. In turn, older children object to studying with those younger and often call them babies. Even at five or six some children will ask to be placed in another class if the majority of the group is only a year younger.

All children and young people are invited to join the People's Art Center and are admitted in the order of application until classes are filled. No child is admitted or rejected on the basis of art ability.

Although all classes carry a tuition fee, there are a number of full and partial scholarships available, approximately one to each class. Scholarships are given on the basis of the child's interest and the family's financial status. No scholarship is presented for superior achievement, talent or special ability. Applications are made in writing by the parent or teacher or by the student himself. Each student is interviewed by the Director and is asked to show a portfolio of not more than a dozen examples of his work (including three-dimensional pieces if he has them). Some of the work should have been done at home completely on his own.

Every class includes both two- and three-dimensional expression—painting, clay work, collage, construction.

Opaque watercolors called "tempera" or "poster colors" are the paints used. Oils are not used in children's classes nor are they favored as a medium for children because they are too sophisticated. They are difficult for the child to control and slow in drying; it is hard to change the color quickly, and the paints are expensive for school or home use. Opaque water colors, with the advantages of oil paints, dry quickly, can be painted over easily, and are economical. Crayons are not favored as a general medium because they are widely used at home and at school and we think it advisable to introduce children to new and more flexible media. Also, crayons are limited in ability to cover an area with rich color. They do not mix easily so that a child can invent new colors, and cannot be changed once they have been applied. Other materials used are colored chalks and inks; and certain graphic processes are employed by older children, such as monoprint, linoleum and wood block.

Among the three-dimensional materials, an inexpensive, nonfiring moist clay is the best plastic medium for children of all ages. Because it is easy to mold and responds readily even to tiny fingers, it can be used by the youngest children. Other materials such as the self-hardening clay are not practical because they are costly, rapid-drying and have an unpleasant tactile quality.

Collage and construction have become "musts" in three-dimensional work for children. Basically, these include such materials as swatches of cloth and paper, both plain and figured, tissue paper, cellophane in various colors, swab sticks, tongue depressors, wire of different gauges, and a variety of materials which may be found in one's own home—buttons, yarn, colored string, bottle caps, net bags for oranges or onions, perforated inserts from vitamin pill boxes and corrugated board; or materials found in one's environment, such as leaves, pebbles, bark, sand and shells. While the teacher or parent may provide some of the staples, for instance, colored paper for tacking or pasting collage material; or cardboard shirtbacks or box covers, net, cellophane, tissue, and so forth; the most important factor is the child's adventure of looking for and finding things himself. Photographs of children's collages and constructions shown in this book will suggest applications for the above materials.

While children are given the opportunity for wide individual choice, there is considerable motivation by the teachers according to the specific requirements of each age level. The laissez-faire approach in which children are given materials and left completely alone without guidance is not approved because it has been discovered that children lack the experience to motivate themselves continuously and to differentiate between creative and noncreative expression. When left alone, children often repeat themselves or tend to imitate the clichés and stereotypes they see in comic books, motion pictures or television programs. Each class, therefore, has a general progressive program which allows for a variety of choices flexible enough to permit any change inspired by current group or individual interests.

It is important that the child's aim or objective be beyond his reach. The work needs to be challenging so that he will exert himself. To insure growth, projects are made progressively more challenging to call for deeper thought and greater skill. Group motivation is commonly used by the teachers to stimulate creative response and to bring about interaction between children, who learn a great deal from each other.

Because teachers are individuals too, with different personalities and special abilities, no two work alike. Each teacher is free to develop his classes in his own way and to use the processes which are most natural to him and most successful with his children. Yet there is a marked

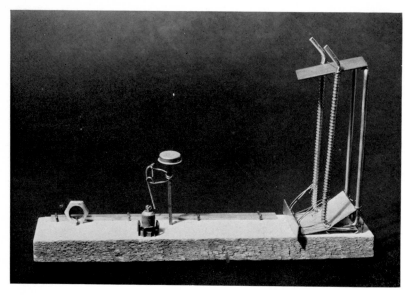

Construction, by Susan, 11½ years

Crazyland Amusement Park, by John, 7 years

Boy making construction.   photo Marion Palfi

Fishing Boat and Dock, by Dennis, 6 years

integration among the teachers because of fundamental agreement on philosophy and method of teaching. As a result, when a child moves on from one teacher to another, there is no feeling of conflict between the two experiences, only a progression of learning and the stimulation of a new personality.

Another major objective is to broaden the child's experience beyond his own personal expressions to include an understanding and enjoyment of the work of mature artists of the present and of the past. This may be accomplished at the younger levels in a variety of ways. Color reproductions and small sculptures may be introduced as part of the class environment, hung upon walls or placed about the room. The teacher may casually call attention to these works or discuss them informally with a single child or a group; they are often used as motivation for creative activity. If the class is interested in doing portraits, the teacher may show a variety by such artists as Picasso, Modigliani, Chagall, Rouault and van Gogh to demonstrate that there is no one way to do a portrait, that the possibilities are infinite and depend on individual inventiveness and will. Motivation may also stem from subject matter, animals or people interesting to a particular age level.

Because they can rationalize and enjoy the analytical process, a more conscious approach to appreciation is employed with older children. Artists, movements, and concepts are discussed and studied directly. Groups may go into the adjoining Museum to study the Collection or current exhibitions. To facilitate general understanding of art and to develop the habit of museum visiting, each child is issued a pass for two which may be used an unlimited number of times during the school term. Few children will visit the Museum by themselves; the extra pass assures more frequent visits and also enlightenment of the companion. When the parent is the companion, a usual situation is reversed: here the child becomes host. It is common in the Museum galleries to see a child of eight or ten espousing theories of modern art or pointing out his favorite painting to his father or mother.

Girl making mobile.   photo Len Ross

Some basic construction materials

Children are never made to copy the paintings or sculpture, the practice in some museums. They are not asked to make diagrams or to take notes. The primary object is to look and enjoy.

In these various ways, what used to be called "art appreciation," tediously memorizing information under the watchful eye of the teacher, becomes a dynamic independent adventure. While this study is devoted to the development of modern art with particular emphasis on the contemporary period, it is by no means restricted to it. The arts of the past are also introduced as background or as roots of the expression of our time.

PHILOSOPHY AND METHOD OF TEACHING ADULTS

The adult classes are planned particularly to satisfy the amateur who has discovered an interest in art. The term "amateur" is used here in its original meaning, one who pursues art for the love of it rather than as a profession. Most adults join the classes because of a leisure-time interest, a desire to create expressively, a wish to broaden cultural horizons, or for all three reasons. The majority of the students are professional people, doctors, lawyers, business men, accountants, office workers and homemakers. A few actors, dancers, writers, teachers, and students are also included. About one-third are men. The age range is from thirty to sixty years, with a smattering of younger and older students, the oldest in their eighties. Professional artists and commercial artists and designers often take the classes for refresher training.

Work from adult classes

A NEW AND UNIQUE TYPE OF STUDENT

The amateur presents an unique and new problem in art education. He chooses art because of a certain felt desire or need. As he was not found in any number a decade or more ago, there were then no methods of developing his interest. To be sure, amateurs with a keen desire for art study or participation did exist, but they were inclined to be occasional individuals whose interest was of long standing, perhaps going back to college or high school. There were also dilettantes who painted because it was fashionable or who studied art in order to be able to discuss it at the dinner table and at cocktail parties. We do not have dilettantes in the Center today.

It is likely that today's amateur recently discovered art, desires to pursue it earnestly for his own satisfaction, and is modest or even timid. Usually he has not studied art or had any contact with it since his school days. Many of our students have never held a brush or other art tool before coming to the Center. The amateur is different in another important way. Students in other schools and situations are captive audiences with an end reward in view. Children go to school and then graduate; older students go to college and receive a diploma or degree; others go to art or professional schools: when art is offered to all of these it is as part of a required curriculum. The amateur alone comes to art classes because of the simple desire for satisfaction; he remains only if that satisfaction is provided. His innocence and his deep desire provide a challenge for the teacher.

Fortunately, the staff of the People's Art Center had acquired a considerable amount of experience in teaching veterans during the four years of the War Veterans' Art Center, which preceded the Center and was also sponsored by the Museum of Modern Art.* The veterans were similar to the amateurs in most respects except, perhaps, for an even more intense desire and earnestness. Techniques were devised in those years, some by trial and error, some by experimentation, which were a great asset in developing teaching for the amateur, the foundation for our present philosophy and method.

Adults are offered about thirty different courses in the categories of orientation, painting, life, sculpture, ceramics, drawing and graphic expression, fundamentals of design, jewelry making, mosaic making, glass as a creative medium, art appreciation, and criticism in painting and in photography. The basic aesthetic concepts and teaching methods of the courses are new, but these courses have familiar "subject" titles for the lay student. (For example, a course called "Experiences in Two- and Three-Dimensional Design" failed to attract students at first because the title was too strange.)

Courses are graded in experience or difficulty and are titled "Painting I," "Painting II," "Painting III," and so forth, or "Ceramics for Beginners" and "Ceramics for Advanced Students." In addition, a paragraph in the catalog describes the content and method of each course. This assists the student in making a choice and places him in a group of students with similar backgrounds. If he wishes, he may also secure the advice of the Director or an instructor in making his selection.

Most beginners know which field or subject they wish to explore, whether painting or ceramics. Some students, however, have only the desire to create but do not know which particular direction or medium they wish to follow. A special course was devised for them called "Orientation", based on a similar one used successfully with the war veterans.

The Orientation Course gives the student an opportunity to find his own special, current interest, and at the same time provides a grounding in the fundamentals of design. The student explores a number of art concepts and media both in two- and three-dimensional materials. While the course does not pretend to discover latent talent or permanent aptitudes, it does effectively enable the student to find his greatest readiness, and it starts him off with a feeling of security. After completion, the student elects any of the more specialized courses.

* cf. *Art for War Veterans,* Museum of Modern Art Bulletin, September, 1954, Vol. XIII, No. 1.

Oil painting by adult

Top: Wood sculpture class

Bottom: Demonstration of pottery throwing on the wheel

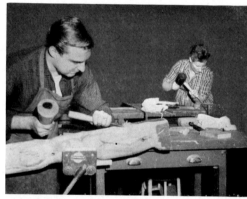

Students tend to continue in the field which they choose at that time. The success of the Orientation Course has been demonstrated by the fact that the classes have grown in number while continuing to serve their basic function.

The main obstacle beginners face is initial fear that they have no talent, that one must have talent in order to succeed, that they may expose themselves to criticism or ridicule by others.

The instruction, therefore, is planned to be simple and to allow a measure of success to be attained at the outset. The major emphasis is on freeing the individual and establishing his confidence. There are a variety of ways to achieve these goals but the general procedure is to introduce simple concepts and techniques which the student can grasp and command. Projects must involve a progression of interest and a challenge so that the student can recognize and evaluate his own growth from week to week or month to month. If he feels he is progressing, he is almost certain to continue; but if he sees no progress, he is likely to drop out of class. A teacher can easily count his failures by the number of students who do not return.

The main objective is to assure satisfaction while maintaining a high standard of perception and achievement. Adults are inclined to follow clichés and stereotypes just as children are; but, unlike children, they are much more inhibited; they tend to dislike the naive and sensitive qualities which are vital to their creative growth. Even when they overcome clichés and stereotypes, many secretly admire these and some even feel that there are short cuts or "tricks of the trade" which the instructor is withholding from them. Thus, the teaching is a constant process of provoking the student to his highest degree of sensitive thinking, to assure a measure of recognizable success, to maintain growth and the ability to evaluate it. While it may be more difficult to teach the amateur than the art school or college student, it is more rewarding because of his great enthusiasm and his deep gratification with the slightest degree of success.

All the adult courses aim not to produce artists but to develop more aesthetically-sensitive individuals who will derive greater pleasure and understanding from the work of artists of the past and present. It was feared by some of the Trustees of the Museum, when the idea of offering practical courses was first suggested, that beginners might feel their naive efforts were as subtle as Klee's or as spontaneous as Kandinsky's. The opposite proved to be the case: many adults were able to understand the aesthetic qualities of such painters for the first time, with a resulting increase in respect and enjoyment.

In addition to the practical courses, the Center offers others which develop appreciation of art more directly. These include "Old Masters to Moderns" and "An Understanding of Modern Art Based on the Museum Collections and Current Exhibitions."

In the ten or more years since the adult classes began, there has been a gratifying degree of success. Thousands of students have completed the courses satisfactorily; so many have wished to continue that more advanced courses have been added. For those who have developed sufficient independence to work on their own, criticism classes have been introduced for periodic analysis and discussion of their work. The classes have acquired such wide attention that educators come from all over the country and from abroad to observe and study. Many have adapted particular courses or have patterned new schools and art centers on the People's Art Center.

Success has, however, produced its own problems. Many students who have achieved considerable proficiency and whose work may have outstanding characteristics begin to look for the recognition or the rewards of the professional artist, exhibiting or selling. While indeed many amateurs may achieve a professional status, and while no one should be denied the privilege of trying, for most people such a goal proves frustrating. Difficulty arises when the amateur attempts to compete with the professional or when he expects the same degree of attention from less effort and experience. Perhaps there should be more opportunity for him to compare his experiences and to show his achievements on his own level.

It must be recognized that the amateur artist and amateur art constitute positive elements in our cultural family; to overlook or suppress this may detract from our culture. But the concept that the pursuit of art, the experience of creating, the evaluation of one's creative self, are the best and most permanent reward, must be emphasized. If this is kept in view, art will continue to nourish the spirit and to make life richer; and all other rewards will be secondary or unimportant by contrast. The ultimate aim for all who pursue art is satisfaction and discovery, not badges or prizes. This is also the test of the truly creative artist.

CONTINUITY IN CREATIVE GROWTH
Vacation Art Classes for Children and Adults

Summer comes with its intense heat and other discomforts, and the city dweller turns his attention to the seashore and the country. Vacation means a holiday from school for the children and at least two weeks' respite from routine work for the adult. For both it often interrupts the continuity of creative growth. While this may not necessarily be a handicap, it often imposes a delay on those who wish to continue their art interests or to combine art experiences with play. Instead of sending their children to camp, many parents would prefer to share their vacation with them but lack ways of finding mutually interesting activities. Furthermore, in most camps the art work is treated superficially and consists of inferior or useless "arts and crafts" projects which undermine any good, creative teaching the children may have had at school.

In consideration of these problems, the Museum of Modern Art established art classes for children and adults on eastern Long Island.

ADULT CLASSES – *Outdoor Painting*

In the summer of 1955 the first Landscape Painting class was opened to adults; the group of more than thirty students ranged in age from twenty-five to seventy. The class painted out-of-doors in a natural environment, returning on Saturday mornings to the studio in The Springs for general wall criticism.

There were at least two major differences from the typical summer painting classes or art schools. One, these students were all amateurs and not a mixture of "artists," professional and perennial students fixed in their ways and styles of painting, an assortment often found in summer classes. This made for a homogeneous and integrated group. Another difference was that the object of this class was to develop individual creativeness and not to concentrate on landscape painting *per se*. The subject matter was merely a point of departure, which the student could interpret or from which he could deviate as he chose. As a result, the expression ran the gamut from realistic to abstract to naive interpretations. The opportunity to concentrate on painting several hours at a time, day after day, resulted in high enthusiasm and a facility of expression seldom achieved in a class which meets only two or three hours a week.

The benefits of this class were social, or perhaps spiritual, as well as creative. The concentrated hours of working together, of learning to evaluate one's own progress as well as that of the group, developed an objective and friendly attitude. A majority of the students continued to work together throughout the year and returned to the class summer after summer. There was little or no competitive spirit because students learned to recognize and respect their own creative individuality as well as that of others, at the same time giving credit to superior achievement. The instructor held no student up as a model for others to follow, nor did he allow students to imitate his own expression and technique or to emulate any professional artist.

Painting on location

Outdoor criticism

photo Maurice Berezov

CLASSES FOR PARENTS AND CHILDREN

The following summer, in 1956, classes for parents and children were set up in a small building in East Hampton. While the teaching was similar to that in the People's Art Center, there was a greater range in the ages of the children, from three to ten years instead of three to five. This wider span worked out successfully, partly because the parents, being on vacation, were freer and more relaxed than in the city, and also perhaps because they were more used to sharing experiences with their children. Independent classes for older children were also given with equal success.

Although summer vacation classes for children, for parents and children, and for adults have continued with success each summer, they are regarded as still in an experimental stage. The possibility of making the vacation a creative adventure for the lay adult, of making it a focus for enriched family life and a heightened experience for the older child and teen-ager, are tremendous and exciting. The potentialities are yet to be discovered.

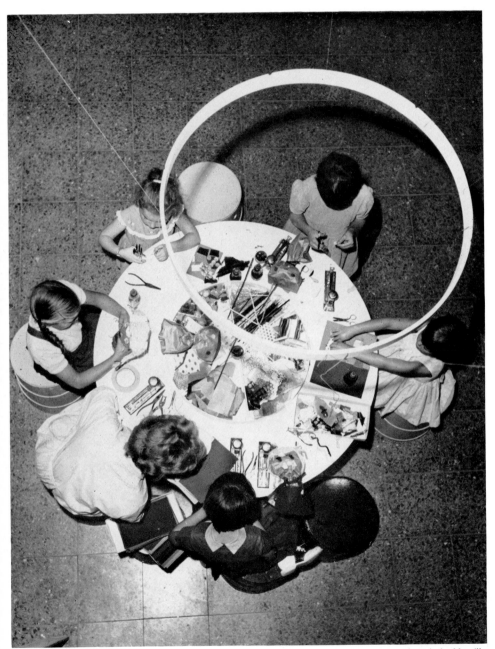

photo Andre Monville

PART III

Children Can Be Creative the World Over

The Children's Carnival of Modern Art

33

The Children's Carnival of Modern Art, a dramatic demonstration of art education, has proved that children can be developed creatively the world over. This experiment in creative teaching has tapped the imaginations of thousands of children and fired the interest of millions of the lay public who watched it at the Museum of Modern Art for the past sixteen years, and in Europe, where it was part of the World's Fair in Brussels and of the International Trade Fairs in Italy and Spain. By the simple means of showing how children respond to art experiences under ideal teaching in a stimulating environment, it has overcome the need of verbal exposition and lengthy argument. The Carnival has further demonstrated that art can be taught to children effectively through television. Under the title "Through the Enchanted Gate," two series of programs successfully reached children individually in their homes and in the schools; these programs will be discussed later in detail.

THE CHILDREN'S CREATIVE CENTER
AT THE BRUSSELS WORLD'S FAIR

If one visited the United States Pavilion at the World's Fair in Brussels, he could hardly have missed the art exhibitions which proved so controversial here at home. But unless he noticed one of the small structures on the second floor with portholes and a sign reading "Children's Creative Center," he would have missed the most exciting and successful art event for children at the Fair. Here, thousands of children from all over the world were introduced to creative teaching; they played with inspiring toys and indulged their imaginations through painting and through making collages and constructions under the guidance of teachers sent from the Museum of Modern Art. For spectators, the natural interest of watching people at work and the fascination of seeing children absorbed in creative experience combined toward its appeal.

Omnibus, the Ford television program, devoted fifteen minutes of its May 4, 1958 telecast to a tour of the Fair;

the Children's Creative Center was considered important enough to focus on for two minutes and twenty-five seconds, a considerable length of time in television. Alistair Cooke, in his introductory remarks, described the essence of this creative oasis for children in the maelstrom of sophisticated adult exhibitions. "One American triumph which will rock no headlines is a play hall that is heaven for the children of all nations and, except you become as a little child, you may no wise enter therein. This is a place where any child may find new uses for a length of string, where he may indulge very simple sensations, like the movement of a caterpillar, like the feel of a cat. Once they have loosened up their imaginations, they move into the inner room [the studio-workshop]."

In Brussels, the Carnival was in operation for the entire six months of the Fair; 16,472 children from all over the world took part in it; more than 2,000 teachers visited the Center; the number of visitors who watched through the portholes or from the gallery above the studio-workshop is incalculable. Only educators and the press were admitted inside.

The Children's Creative Center was the same as the Children's Carnival of Modern Art, for sixteen years the major event for children at the Museum of Modern Art. A description of the general program follows.

THE CARNIVAL IN OPERATION

The Carnival plan consists of two areas or galleries, the first for motivating the child, the second for his participation in an art activity. After being motivated or inspired by the different toys and games and perhaps relieved of some of the clichés and stereotypes with which his mind is often burdened, the child enters the Studio-Workshop, which is the Participation Area. Here he is invited to make a painting, a collage, or a construction, or all three if he wishes; and he is guided in his efforts by experienced teachers.

In addition to its function as a new and effective kind

of demonstration of creative teaching, the Carnival presents contemporary design dramatically, to appeal to the child, the parent, and the educator. For the child, it is a world of fantasy created for him alone. For the parent, it is a private window looking into the child's creative life, through which to watch the art process evolve; for the educator, it offers new ideas and methods of teaching and shows new and varied materials and equipment.

At the entrance to the Carnival is the Contour Gate, a white metal rod curved in the shape of two children, a four-year-old and a twelve-year-old, the age limits of those admitted. This has become the famous symbol of the Carnival and is used wherever it goes. It is a tactful reminder that the Carnival is only for children, that only those who can fit through the gate without crouching may enter. Adults and older children, who might otherwise become indignant or arrogant at being kept out, are amused and sometimes delighted with the ingenuity of the device. A place for viewing from the outside is always provided. In the Museum of Modern Art there is a fence on which parents may lean to watch their children; in Europe glassed panels or portholes were used. Adults are not admitted into the Carnival for three reasons. First, psychologically, it is designed as a child's world; this is pleasing to children and stimulates independent activity. Second, it removes the child from parental interference or domination. Parents often tend to hover over their children's work, making suggestions or criticisms. Third, the presence of too many adults is confusing to the child and is not conducive to concentration. Educators and the press are the only exceptions made, and they are requested not to interrupt the children or to interfere with any activity.

INSPIRATIONAL AREA

Once through the Contour Gate, the child finds himself in the Inspirational Area. This is a semi-darkened room painted in deep blues and greens with toys either in pools of light or lighted from within, giving a jewel-like effect.

The mood intended is one of magic and fantasy, of a friendly forest, cool and quiet, with delightful surprises beckoning the child from every direction. The cheerful mood is emphasized by a continuous background of musical recordings of such selections as "The Nutcracker Suite" and "Swan Lake" by Tchaikovsky, Ferde Grofé's "Grand Canyon Suite," and the "Hansel and Gretel Suite" by Humperdinck.

The Inspirational Area provides a new approach to art teaching, for here the child is stimulated to think creatively and is oriented to the fundamentals of design without words or dogma of any kind. Unique toys or devices originated by outstanding designers involve the child in aesthetic concepts of color, texture, and rhythm. The *Color Player*, an instrument constructed like a piano with keys and pedals, permits the child to project continuous moving patterns on a screen in front of him. Another toy, the *Feeling Cat*, stimulates the child's tactile sense. Here a wide steel band, made in the shape of a cat and covered with fur, arches its back when a child strokes it. The *Magnetic Picture Maker* is a magnetized panel set in a frame, on which the child can freely arrange designs with geometric and free-form shapes and bird and animal contours. Designs can be improvised spontaneously without the worry of making mistakes or erasing because they can be moved about or replaced instantly. A *Game Table* has jigsaw puzzles made from color reproductions of paintings by modern artists who are favorites of children, paintings such as Camille Bombois's "Before Entering the Ring," Chagall's "I and the Village," and Picasso's "The Three Musicians." The *Giant Builder* is a series of slotted wooden rectangles which fit together ingeniously so that one or more children can make abstract structures resembling modern architecture; it is based on the cantilever principle of an occult or offset balance. The *Space Ship Design Projector*, the largest mechanism in the gallery, which two children can operate at the same time, is a life-size toy constructed to suggest a space ship. It has dials, steering gears and pedals.

Three spotlights behind color discs project moving patterns of color on to suspended forms, which suggest planets, and a curved cyclorama behind. Here the children can imagine they are flying through space as they are stimulated by the changing colors and moving patterns. (See Page 39 for a detailed description of the toys.)

STUDIO-WORKSHOP AREA

As the children leave the Inspirational Area and go into the Studio-Workshop, they emerge into a different atmosphere, brilliantly lighted and painted in gay, warm colors. Here, against walls of Chinese vermilion, chartreuse or blue-green, are cantilevered easels in contrasting colors set at different heights or adjustable to the convenient working position of any child. (For example, yellow easels are placed against red walls or blue easels against yellow.) In the center of the gallery two round white collage tables (or, as in some earlier designs, one long table) are spotlighted from above. In the center of the tables are lazy-susans or turntables with pie-shaped divisions filled with stimulating materials such as colored feathers, pipe cleaners, sequins, colored and patterned papers, and cloth. Above each table is suspended a hoop, or some other device, from which the children hang mobiles as they make them. Mobiles by artists are hung in both galleries to give the Carnival a festive and enchanting air.

A child spends from an hour to an hour and a half in the Carnival, depending on his interest span and the convenience of the schedule. About one-third of the time is spent in the Inspirational Area and two-thirds in the Studio-Workshop. A child may make two or three paintings and a collage or a construction, or both, in the time. The things he makes are his property and he takes them away with him.

Children are left to work independently. A child is assisted by a teacher only when he does not know how to operate a toy, how to get started on a collage or construction, or when he does not seem to be deriving all the satisfaction possible from a given experience.

Entering through Contour Gate

View of Inspirational Area, table with toys on left. photo Van der Veen

Studio-Workshop Area in Brussels World's Fair

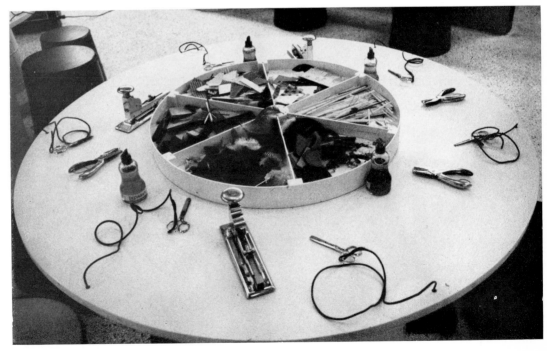

Close-up of collage table with tools and lazy-susan in center.   photo Van der Veen

Gallery of Toys in the Children's Creative Center,
United States Pavilion, Brussels World's Fair.
Presented by The Museum of Modern Art, New York

5. photo Van de

1. photo Van der Veen

2.

3. photo Van der Veen

4.

7.

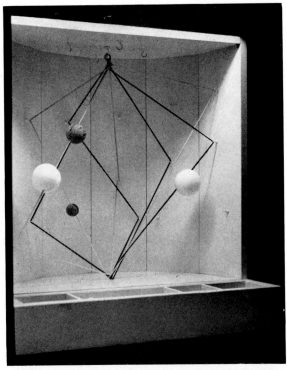

1. *Furry Cat.* A sculptured shape, arches back when petted. Part of the Fantasy Zoo—three toys designed by Ruth Vollmer.

2. *Design Color Window.* Based on principle of stained glass window. By placing variously-shaped colored plexiglas in front of three shallow strips on a lighted plexiglas sheet, an infinite variety of colors and designs are produced. Specially designed for the Fair by Victor D'Amico.

3. *Magnetic Board.* By placing colored abstract and representational shapes on the white surface of the magnetic board, the child visualizes many arrangements of color and pattern. Designed by Leonard Nelson.

4. *Space Ship Projector.* To stimulate space travel in the imagination, two children, in cockpit-like toy, transmit color patterns to a screen by operating steering wheels, pedals and panel switches. Three projectors produce effects: light passes through colored gelatins and other materials sandwiched between plastic discs; these may be changed like phonograph records, with an almost endless variety of results. Designed by Victor D'Amico.

5. *Color Players.* Involves "painting with light"; one player fitted with cool colors, a second with warm. On two tree-like structures in a large box, child hangs abstract shapes, bird and animal forms. With a window lowered in front of the box, child changes colors shining on trees by punching four different keys; adds motion by revolving trees with foot pedals. Designed by Victor D'Amico.

6. *Three-Dimensional String Design.* The child attaches six pieces of elastic string, fixed at one end in a large shadow box, to a choice of hooks in walls and ceiling of the box. He then hangs three-dimensional decorations on the strings. Designed by Victor D'Amico.

7. *String Picture Makers.* Horizontal and vertical elastics spaced on peg boards produce designs when the child inserts golf tees into holes and brings elastics around them. A small size designed for the individual child; a large one for two or three to work together. Designed by Victor D'Amico.

8. *Giant Builder.* An adaptation of the small Builder toy first introduced in a 1953 Museum exhibition of toys. Now produced commercially. Enlarged size permits two or more children to work together. Designed by A. F. Arnold.

Carnival in Milan. photo Van der Veen

Carnival in Barcelona

THE CARNIVAL: A WORLD-FAMOUS INSTITUTION

In addition to the recognition it received at the Brussels Fair, in 1957 the Carnival, under the auspices of the United States Department of Commerce, was the focus of attention at the International Trade Fairs in Milan and Barcelona.

Both in Italy, where it was called "Il Paradiso dei Bambini" (The Children's Paradise), and in Spain as "El Festival de Arte de los Niños" (The Children's Art Festival), the Carnival was a distinct success. At every hour of the day it was filled to capacity. It furnished another example of art as a universal language: regardless of nationality, children immediately comprehended its meaning and participated freely. Through the glass windows thousands of visitors watched the children at work, and they often queued for blocks outside the Pavilion, waiting to get in. The press, television, and movies gave special attention to the Carnival and welcomed it as an outstanding contribution of the United States. As one Italian reporter stated, "What better way is there to develop a feeling of brotherhood between nations than to minister to the interests and needs of their children?"

No other single activity of the Museum's Department of Education has received so much public notice consistently, year after year. Both through visiting teachers and the press, the ideas, methods, and equipment of the Carnival have been adopted entirely or in part all over the world.

SOME CONSIDERATIONS OF EDUCATIONAL SIGNIFICANCE

Two important factors emerge from the various experiments of the Children's Carnival. First, that children can be developed creatively regardless of their previous background. In hundreds of instances children who had no art training whatever or who had been taught under the most academic and indoctrinary methods responded quickly to the freedom and dynamic quality of the creative approach. Second, that ethnic or national background has no bearing on the child's creativity. Italian children, for example, are neither more nor less creative than American. Creative children are the result of an education that develops creativeness; uncreative children are the victims of indoctrinary teaching. It is that simple.

photo Barry Kramer

PART IV

Cooperating with Schools in
Producing Visual Materials for the
Teaching of Art; Creative
Opportunities for High School
Students and Elementary School
Teachers

41

THE NEW YORK CITY PUBLIC HIGH SCHOOL PROGRAM

It might seem incongruous if not miraculous that the Museum's successful program of providing visual materials to the largest school system in the world should work out ideally: it would be thought difficult to work intimately and effectively with such an enormously complex organization, yet the partnership has not only endured but has steadily grown stronger throughout the more than twenty years of its existence.

The Board of Education and the High Schools, both part of the gigantic school system of New York City, were among the first to join the Museum's Educational Program in 1937 when it began under a grant from the General Education Board of the Rockefeller Foundation. They alone continued in the program after the expiration of that grant five years later; and they have maintained their interest and cooperation to date, helping to support their participation in the activities.

Not only was an effective program worked out to enrich the teaching of creative art and art appreciation in the city high schools, but the visual materials devised are unique in education and have served the needs of schools everywhere. The program was an experiment in finding new resources to satisfy the creative and cultural interest of the adolescent student, and a practical operation in servicing a growing number of high schools throughout the year.

While the following account is essentially a history of the program carried on between the Museum of Modern Art and the New York City High Schools, it may suggest ways other museums and schools can develop similar activities and also offer ideas to the individual art teacher for evolving visual materials for his own teaching.

There were only three participating public high schools in 1937; today over 130 sets of visual materials consisting of exhibitions, slide talks, teaching models, teaching portfolios, films, or libraries of color reproductions and texts are circulated to at least 58 academic and vocational high schools each month. It was estimated in 1949 that over 175,000 students each year were exposed to these materials, either as observers of exhibitions in school corridors and galleries or as students in classrooms and studios where the models, portfolios or slide talks are used as part of the art curriculum.

Ideas for visual materials are proposed by the Museum; by Miss Olive Riley, Director of Art for the New York City schools; by the chairmen of the high school art departments; and by the teachers who use the materials. Constant evaluation is made jointly by the schools and the Museum to improve the quality and usefulness.

All materials used as teaching aids were designed to meet the varying concepts and interests of the adolescent and to conform with the requirements of a large school system. The Teaching Models, as an example, are packaged instructional materials; each model includes a small exhibition, background texts for the student to read, and units to assemble—a stage set, a room, or a three-dimensional construction—each boxed in a cabinet mounted on rollers so that it can be moved easily from classroom to classroom. Subjects of Teaching Models include neighborhood planning, interior design, costume, abstract design, display, and theater art. The Teaching Portfolio, a series of plates with a text to be used in the classroom, is either set on the chalk tray or bulletin board as a small exhibition or passed around to the students. The Teaching Portfolios published by the Museum in quantity for general distribution include *Modern Sculpture, Texture and Pattern, Modern Art Old and New* and *Useful Objects Today*; they originated in the program for New York City schools.

Lending Libraries are provided so that a student may borrow a color reproduction of a modern painting, take it home and live with it. In doing this, he may perhaps encourage his family to enjoy the work.

Slide Talks, consisting of a text and from twenty-five to forty slides, have been prepared for classroom or assembly use on such topics as "New Forms of Our

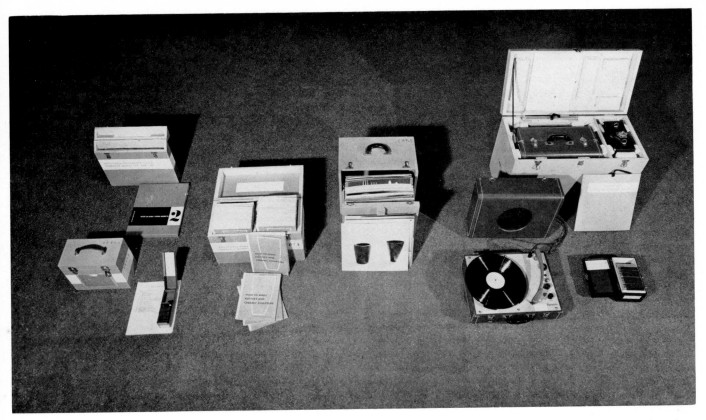

Packaged teaching materials, including teaching portfolio, slide talk, text on pottery making, portable case of photographic plates on useful objects, and recorded slide talk

Time," "Adventure in Modern Art," and "What Is Modern Painting?"

In detail, the program is carried out by the following procedure. Each school receives a choice blank in June describing all the visual materials available for circulation during the following year. As stated previously, the items are grouped in six categories—exhibitions, teaching portfolios or libraries of color reproductions, teaching models, libraries of texts, slide talks, and films. From these, the chairman of the art department, or a teacher appointed to take charge of this program makes several choices in order of preference, and indicates the semester, fall or spring term, when the school would like to have each material. Because of the vast number of selections made and the necessity for economy in transportation, it is not possible to schedule all materials exactly for the particular months desired; but through the flexibility of the New York City art curriculum and the ingenuity of the teachers, instruction can be correlated with the arrival of the materials. To facilitate this, each school receives its schedule for the year at the beginning of the fall term.

Here are typical descriptions of some of the items listed in the choice blank, from which a school makes its selection.

WHAT IS YOUR NEIGHBORHOOD LIKE?

...a neighborhood in Harlem

...a neighborhood in Brooklyn

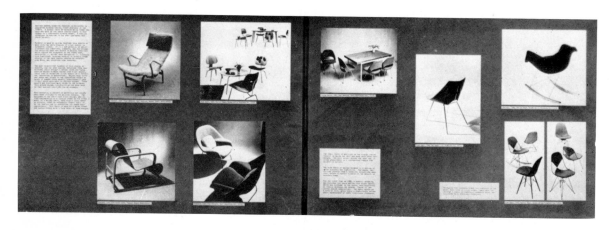

LETTERING

ITS DESIGN

AND

ARRANGEMENT

PREPARED BY THE DEPARTMENT OF EDUCATION, MUSEUM OF MODERN ART, N.Y.

EXHIBITIONS

Art Museums in New York City: 9 panels, 30″ × 40″; 2 panels, 30″ × 20″, approximately 50 running feet—exploring the various art resources in the following museums in the city: the Metropolitan, the Frick, the Guggenheim, the Whitney, the Brooklyn, and the Museum of Modern Art. The object is to encourage high school students to make use of the wealth of art to be found in our city.

You and Your Neighborhood: 24 panels, 24″ × 30″, approximately 90 running feet—an exhibition designed to make the student aware of his neighborhood as a setting for community living. A good neighborhood is described in terms of houses, schools, stores, places of worship, and recreational features. The exhibition does not present an ideal neighborhood but makes comparisons of existing examples of old and new solutions.

TEACHING PORTFOLIO

Modern Design in Furniture: 10 panels, 20″ × 30″, approximately 25 running feet—photographs and labels of explanatory text showing the development of modern furniture design, emphasizing chairs, tables, and storage pieces by such outstanding designers as Eames and Saarinen.

TEACHING MODELS

Design Teaching Model: a variety of geometric solids and geometric and organic shapes painted in various colors, for use in teaching design. A platform and background are provided for setting up compositions. Units and platform fit into a cabinet 28″ high × 37″ wide, which is mounted on rollers so that it can be easily moved about.

Lettering: Its Design and Arrangement: 14 panels, 20″ × 30″, including 3 panels with plastic faces, approximately 45 running feet—cut-out, plastic letters of various sizes, shapes and colors, illustrating major type faces are provided. They can be easily arranged on the plastic panels for experimental exercises. The rest of the panels show various types and arrangements of lettering.

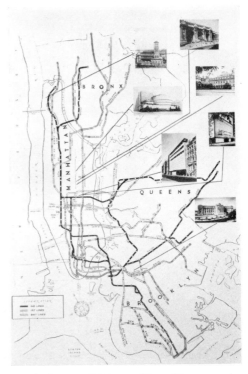

Panel from exhibition "Art Museums in New York City"

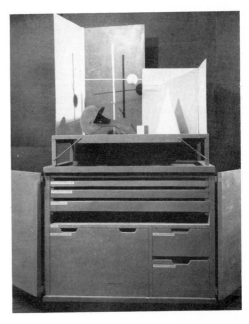

Design teaching model and cabinet

45

In addition to making its choices, each school is asked to evaluate the materials it has received during the previous year on the basis of teaching effectiveness, quality of the art materials included, visual presentation, explanatory text, and ease of handling. The school is also asked to suggest improvements for the existing materials and to propose ideas for new ones. During the summer months, all items are revised in terms of the criticisms made and are refurbished because of wear. Perhaps an example of the effectiveness of the cooperation in planning is the fact that only two items in the twenty-two years of circulation were withdrawn for lack of usefulness. Many materials have, however, been retired after certain periods due to current needs of students and changes in the teaching program. For example, we now use fewer large exhibitions. There is a trend toward smaller displays which can be used in the classroom and passed among students, a trend away from the large spectacular exhibitions hung in the school corridor or in a gallery especially given to the purpose. Another change has been from extensive explanatory texts in paragraph form to simple terse sentences. This is due in part to the influx into the city schools of many foreign-speaking students, whose command of English is limited.

The program is under the personal supervision of the Director of Art, Miss Riley, who reviews all materials and makes suggestions for new ones. She studies the materials with her staff and with the chairmen of the art departments that use the materials. On two occasions, committees have been appointed to evaluate the program and its use in the schools. Miss Riley also meets with the superintendents and principals to describe the educational function of the program and to encourage a wider use of the materials in the schools. Without this personal interest on the part of the Director and the chairmen, the program could never have succeeded so well or perhaps even survived. With regard to the program, Miss Riley says: "The Museum's educational program for our New York public schools has always been a most valuable and dynamic force in supplementing the regular art program in the academic and vocational high schools. These characteristics have been made possible, as the program developed over the years, because its Director, Victor D'Amico, has always been keenly aware of the important factors of suitability, variety, and student interest. His staff, in actively servicing the schools, has always been conscientious and thorough; the material has been delivered promptly and equitably. That these rich and varied materials serve their purpose is clearly shown by the keen interest evinced by the boys and girls who view them."

The program is jointly financed by the Museum and the Board of Education of New York City at a budget of approximately $14,000 per year, half supplied by the City.

While this program is restricted to the schools of New York City, its concepts and visual materials have been adopted by and have provided ideas for many other schools throughout the United States and in many foreign countries. Several of the visual aids such as the Teaching Models and the Teaching Portfolios, which have been published by the Museum and sold extensively, are revolutionary in the field of art education.

Not until the 130 separate items of visual materials are amassed in the Museum's Receiving Room is one aware of the magnitude of the program. Perhaps the most impressive factor is that the largest school system in the world finds modern art important enough to make it a regular part of its curriculum; and it is a tribute to the Director, chairmen, and teachers of this vast and complex organization that they have been and are working closely and effectively with the Museum in producing a successful and dynamic program of visual instruction.

Circulating material on exhibition in warehouse

Neighborhood planning teaching model

SPECIAL SERVICES FOR HIGH SCHOOL STUDENTS

A system introduced into the Museum's high school program many years ago has produced gratifying results. Fifty to one hundred interchangeable student passes to the Museum and annual passes for teachers are given to each of the participating schools. The passes are loaned by the teacher to any student or class, so that hundreds or even thousands from one school may visit the Museum in a year. This has developed the habit of museum visiting; experience has shown that not only do many of the students make use of these passes during their high school years but they continue to come to the Museum when they are in college or art school. Each pass admits two students because it is more agreeable to go with a friend than alone. The teachers' passes similarly induce teachers to come to the Museum more often, and many become Museum members.

In addition, special art classes have been given for especially interested students. Since the number who can be accommodated at the People's Art Center is limited, each public high school in New York City is invited to recommend two students. The classes are filled from the recommended list on the basis of interest and on viewing portfolios of work. This again raises the question of the gifted student. It has been mentioned that there are no adequate methods for identifying the gifted and that the People's Art Center feels that segregating students by any arbitrary means is educationally unwise. Interested students are often selected because their school is unable to offer the amount of specialized study they deserve.

WORKSHOPS FOR ELEMENTARY SCHOOL TEACHERS

Recognizing the need for experienced art instruction for the younger child, the Museum set up art workshops free of charge for New York City elementary school teachers. Through the cooperation of the Director of Art an effective program has been formed which has served as a model for other organizations and communities interested in orientation and refresher courses for grade teachers. The Museum has felt rewarded in seeing how successfully many of the teachers have introduced in their classes the educational concepts and methods stressed in the workshops. The gratification is slight however in consideration of the great need for better art education and for visual materials of good aesthetic quality for this age level; it is a critical area in American education because creative growth and taste are formed in the elementary years. The Museum is restrained in its interest and operation because of limited funds.

PART V

Leadership in Art Education

photo Len Ross

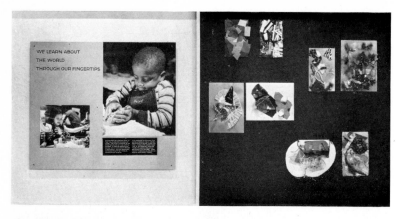

Two panels from exhibition "The Human Quality in Creative Experience"

Installation of Exhibition "The Human Quality in Creative Experience"

Reception at 1951 annual conference, National Committee on Art Education: left, J. B. Neumann and Charles Sheeler; right, Victor D'Amico and Nelson A. Rockefeller.

photos John Langley

THE NATIONAL COMMITTEE ON ART EDUCATION

How and why does a national art organization get started? There are perhaps as many answers as there are organizations in America. The National Committee on Art Education began for at least three particular and serious reasons. First, the founders had no idea of starting an organization: coincidence brought them together when they were restricted in freedom of expression in a meeting of the annual conference of a large art association. Second, they were prompted by their desire to find an organization free of the compromises that had to be made to the business interests on whose support most art organizations depend. Third, they were desirous of organizing a group devoted to education and to excellence in creative teaching at all levels. The group, consisting of less than a dozen individuals, met at the Museum of Modern Art in 1942 to discuss these interests; the formation of the Committee was the result. The primary aim was not only to find a sponsor which would leave them free from commercial or other vested interests, but one which would share their ideals for the advancement of art education, one which represented the most courageous views in contemporary art and the highest achievement in aesthetic standards. The Museum of Modern Art was sympathetic to the Committee's objectives and agreed to become its sponsor. This sponsorship has continued for seventeen years.

The National Committee on Art Education is an organization of leading art directors, supervisors, artists, and teachers of every age level from pre-school through college and art school. While there are many other art organizations in the United States, this Committee is recognized as a spearhead of new ideas in its search for the highest standards of art teaching. From the beginning, it has encouraged sound creative education and has consistently opposed all influences which seek to exploit the child or tend to undermine the values of art education. It was first to expose the danger of contests, copy books, and the paint-by-numbers kits, as it was first to promote better television art programs and improved education for the classroom teacher. Its conferences, exhibitions, and publications produced in cooperation with the Museum of Modern Art have won distinction for the high quality of their teaching objectives and their design. The Committee holds annual meetings in important educational institutions throughout the country and returns about every third year to meet in New York City at the Museum of Modern Art. A theme indicates the aim of each conference; the following selected themes from past conferences indicate the direction of the Committee's thinking.

1945 Art in a Free World
1947 A Search for a Basic Philosophy
1952 Art Education and the Quality of Human Action
1954 Art Education and the Creative Process
1955 The Creative Individual in the Modern World
1957 Education and the Imagination
1958 The Art in Art Education
1959 The Art in Art Education
1960 The Art in Art Education

Constantly on the alert for ways to improve teaching and for any lag or reaction in art education, the Committee, in 1957, issued a statement on the need for a re-evaluation of art education because of the possible decline of aesthetic content due to pressures from other subjects and interests in the school curriculum. The essence of the statement is contained in the following paragraphs:

"While it is true that more art is taught in the schools than ever before, and that there are greater demands for art teachers than can be met, the increased demand is in part due to the increase in school-age population. It does not necessarily follow that more widespread teaching of art has led to better teaching of art.

"More than ever there is a vital need for aesthetic sensitivity in our daily living and in our relationships to environment. It is, therefore, with growing concern that the Council views any attempt to sacrifice art in favor of any other subject."

Major speakers at the 18th annual conference, National Committee on Art Education, left to right: Alfred H. Barr, Jr., Harold Taylor, Robert Iglehart, René d'Harnoncourt

The theme of the conference in 1958, "The Art in Art Education," was chosen as a result of the statement and was considered so vital to the nature of art education that the Council elected to retain this same theme for the following two or three years.

Outstanding speakers have been brought before the Committee to give direction and to stimulate the conference. Among those who have appeared on its platform are Irwin Edman, Walter Gropius, Archibald MacLeish, Margaret Mead, Lewis Mumford, Richard Neutra, Herbert Read and Meyer Schapiro.

Committee membership now includes a majority of distinguished art educators in the United States and Canada, and it is attracting the alert younger teachers from whom will come future leaders. The greatest value of the Committee is not in its leaders but in the leadership of the large group of its members from various regions of the country—town, village, and city—who exchange ideas, discuss teaching experiences, and explore new and better creative methods.

The Committee is endeavoring through conferences, publications, slide talks and exhibitions to make parents and general educators aware of the importance of well-guided creative education for children. In addition to increase of its membership and growth of its activities, the Committee has influenced both art and general education.

The association between the Committee and the Museum has proved valuable in that the Committee undertakes research which enables the Museum to develop new activities, publications, and exhibitions advantageous to both. Notably, three Museum Teaching Portfolios resulted from suggestions made by the Committee Council and a poll taken of its members.

No teacher can be content with his individual endeavor. He needs the cooperation of other art teachers under a guided program. The ivory tower concept of art is obsolete. Art education must help to orient the individual to a world concept of living.

The National Committee on Art Education is an organization with national influence and prestige. It will continue to be an avant-garde group, exploring new techniques while maintaining basic values. Upon this foundation its continuation and growth are assured.

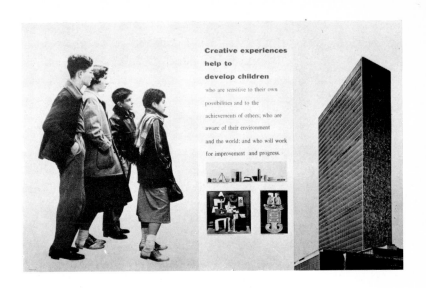

Panels and installation of exhibition "Developing
Creativeness in Children," 13th annual conference,
National Committee on Art Education

COUNCIL OF THE NATIONAL COMMITTEE
ON ART EDUCATION 1958–1959

Chairman: Victor D'Amico

Assistant Chairman: Arthur R. Young

Treasurer: Charles Cook

Secretary: Dorothy Knowles

Representative of the Department of Education of the Museum:
  Victor D'Amico

Council Members:

Alice A. D. Baumgarner
Angiola Churchill
Howard Conant
F. Eleanor Elliott
Robert Iglehart
Dorothy Leadbeater
John Lembach
Lois Lord
Edith L. Mitchell
Ruth Reeves
Olive L. Riley
Hanna T. Rose
Sam G. Weiner
Ralph L. Wickiser
Hale Woodruff

Council Associates:

John V. Allcott, Chapel Hill, North Carolina
Julia H. Duncan, Louisville, Kentucky
August L. Freundlich, Nashville, Tennessee
Boyer Gonzales, Seattle, Washington
Ruth E. Halvorsen, Portland, Oregon
Marion F. T. Johnson, Wilmington, Delaware
Marion E. Miller, Denver, Colorado
Eugenia C. Nowlin, Washington, D.C.
Alice Schoelkopf, Oakland, California

Among past Council Members are:

Jane Cooper Bland
Belle Boas*
Lamar Dodd
Robert Else
Sue Fuller
Florence Harrison
Bartlett H. Hayes, Jr
Ruth R. Herring
Carl E. Hiller
Mervin Jules
Fred Logan
Virginia Murphy*
Harry Sternberg
Jane B. Welling
Dorothy Wilkinson
Robert Wirth   * Deceased

PART VI

Pioneering in Art Education

From kinescope of *Through the Enchanted Gate*

Three scenes from kinescope of
Through the Enchanted Gate

BACKGROUND OF THE DEPARTMENT 1937–1960

The Museum's Department of Education has aimed to pioneer in new directions and to promote better teaching methods in every possible way. This has been demonstrated by the founding of the National Committee on Art Education, in which it played a major role in 1941, and by the establishment of the War Veterans' Art Center, forerunner of the People's Art Center, a significant experiment inspired by the late Mrs. John D. Rockefeller, Jr. and co-sponsored by Mr. Stephen C. Clark from 1944–1948.* The Department began in 1937 as the Educational Project, with a part-time director and a secretary. The program consisted of teaching four high school classes a week, preparing and circulating visual materials to ten high schools, and operating the Young People's Gallery. Today the staff includes a full-time director with six assistants and twenty-four teachers, both full-time and part-time, who carry on the four major activities; the People's Art Center, the Program for New York City High Schools, the Children's Carnival of Modern Art, and the cooperation with the National Committee

* Museum of Modern Art Bulletin, Sept. 1945, Volume XII, No. 1.

on Art Education. In addition, the Department answers hundreds of letters from parents and teachers and meets with numerous visitors from all over the world who are interested in the Museum or who wish to discuss problems of art education.

TELEVISION – *Through the Enchanted Gate*

In 1952 and 1953, the Department of Education produced the successful television series *Through the Enchanted Gate*, under the combined sponsorship of the Museum of Modern Art and the National Broadcasting Company. This was an experiment in teaching art to children at home through the television screen. There were two series of thirteen weekly half-hour shows each, written, produced, and carried out by the staff of the Department of Education and the teachers of the People's Art Center, who appeared "live" in front of the camera. The first series was for children three through ten years of age; the second series included parents as well as children.

The format of the half-hour programs, similar in both series, was unique. All shows were produced in the National Broadcasting Company studio with Ben Grauer as commentator. He and the producer introduced the theme of the show each week, describing the activity to be explored and the materials to be used. The camera then opened on the children going through the Enchanted Gate (the same famous Contour Gate in the Children's Carnival) and followed them to the workshop, where the teacher discussed with them the work to be done. The children, from the People's Art Center classes, then proceeded to tables and began their projects: their part of the program was completely unrehearsed. They did creative work spontaneously and naturally before the television camera. The camera panned across each child as he started, returned to the producer and then to a single child who repeated the motivation given by the teacher for the children at home, so that they might begin work at will. The camera then picked up the teacher and Ben Grauer in the role of an interested layman. Together they reviewed each child's work, and the teacher explained the aims and procedure. While the children were finishing their projects, the camera returned to the producer who gave advice to the parents on how to develop their children's creative interests at home, or discussed the work mailed in by the home audience. The program closed with the children coming out through the Enchanted Gate carrying their work, and Ben Grauer announcing the project and materials for the next week.

The second series, called *Art for the Family*, included parents who appeared in the program and worked along with their children. A change was made in reviewing the work. The teacher discussed the work with each child without the commentator and the producer reviewed the work of the parents.

The program was immediately successful with both parents and teachers. Hundreds of letters were received, endorsing the program and asking particular questions about education. John Crosby, television editor for the *New York Herald-Tribune*, wrote: "There should be more of this kind of television which makes demands on the children whose imaginations are in danger of being throttled rather than stimulated by TV."

A survey was made of over 600 parents who had written in, to evaluate the program. The results of the survey and the work sent in demonstrated that children are able to learn both concepts and techniques and to produce creative work of merit through television. The survey further revealed that only a few children worked while the show was in progress. Most of them watched the program to the end and did their own work im-

mediately afterward or later in the week. Teachers were especially pleased with the program and many of them used the projects in their own teaching, or had children work on the project in class after they had been motivated through the television series.

Kinescopes were made of all programs and a number are now being circulated to schools by the Film Library of the Museum of Modern Art.

Subjects and Themes of Through the Enchanted Gate

First Series, Children 3–10 years

Make a Feeling Picture
Make a Feeling and Seeing Picture*
Discover What You Can Do with Paint
Paint How You Feel Inside
Paint a Picture of Sounds*
Paint What You Know and Imagine
Tell Your Ideas with Clay*
Make an Imaginary Paper Animal
Make Paper Magics*
Space Designs*
Space Designs That Move
Let's Have a Circus Party
Do What You Like Best

Second Series, Art for the Family

Family Pets
Family Portraits*
Paint What You Hear
City-Inspired*
Relating Material to the Idea
Easter Parade
Up in the Sky*
Under the Sea*
Sound and Feeling of Weather
Creating from Memory
In Touch with Your World*

Rain, painting by child, an example of home audience participation in the television show *Through the Enchanted Gate*

* Indicates kinescopes which are circulated by the Film Library of the Museum of Modern Art.

A family art gallery

RESEARCH AND STUDY PROGRAM

A special study program was inaugurated in 1955 to explore problems in teaching art and to circulate the findings to teachers and schools through reports, publications, and visual aids. The first project undertaken was to investigate the effects of clichés and stereotypes on children's work. Selected examples from the New Lincoln School, an outstanding private school in New York City, were studied under the direction of Mrs. Jean d'Autilia, a staff member of the People's Art Center. The study was conducted in a unique manner. First, each teacher of the People's Art Center staff independently evaluated the children's art work on a written form. The evaluations were tabulated. Then, the children's work and the results of the tabulations were discussed by the Director and the staff, and these discussions were recorded on tape. Mrs. d'Autilia's article was based on the discussions and the tabulations and was published in mimeographed form.

Copies may be purchased from the Department of Education.

A second study now under way deals with children's preferences in paintings. Under the direction of Mrs. Jane Cooper Bland, it will bring up to date an earlier study made by the Museum of Modern Art and the National Committee on Art Education. The study is made with color reproductions, not only to determine children's preferences in paintings of the present and the past, but to prepare a list of available reproductions which can be used by teachers or purchased for the school and home.

Other studies under way are:

Classes for Parents and Children, supervised by Moreen Maser

New Techniques in Two- and Three-Dimensional Design, by Margaret Stark

Experiments in Glass, by Priscilla Porter

Children playing with jigsaw puzzle made from Museum color reproduction

Free-standing easel

DESIGNED FOR CHILDREN

A special interest of the Department of Education lies in design and stems partly from the Carnival. Parents and educators have been encouraged to provide a stimulating place for the child to work, to purchase better designed toys and art equipment for the school and home; manufacturers have been encouraged to produce well-designed products of this kind. The effort began long before the study program was inaugurated and is now part of the program. Examples of easels, art sets, collage and construction kits and jigsaw puzzles were exhibited in the Young People's Gallery of the Museum of Modern Art. Many of them were produced by the Department of Education and have been sold from time to time to test their usefulness and to improve their design. But since the Museum neither wishes nor is prepared to go into a production field, these items were not continued. As new toys and furniture are designed, information will be released for the benefit of art education.

PUBLICATIONS OF THE DEPARTMENT OF EDUCATION

Art for the Family, by Victor D'Amico, Frances Wilson, and Moreen Maser

Art of the Young Child—Three to Five Years, by Jane Cooper Bland (Research Program Publication)

How To Make Modern Jewelry, by Charles Martin in collaboration with Victor D'Amico

How To Make Objects of Wood, by Kendall T. Bassett and Arthur B. Thurman in collaboration with Victor D'Amico

How To Make Pottery and Ceramic Sculpture, by Julia Hamlin Duncan and Victor D'Amico

photo Hella Hammid

PART VII

Evaluation

A report is of necessity an evaluation. The increase in activities over the years, the growth in the number of individuals who have been satisfied, the extension of services beyond the Museum, are all evidences of achievement. Yet one is conscious that the American tendency is to measure success by quantity and size and to overlook the intangibles of quality. It is, of course, difficult to convey or measure the expressions of delight on the faces of the thousands of children who attended the Carnival or to say exactly what beyond the finished work a child takes home from an art class of the People's Art Center, although the instructors are certain that a wonderful and vital transformation takes place in him during the term. One cannot tell how profoundly the materials sent to the New York City schools affect individual students, even though the teachers declare that these materials are indispensable to their work; or what it is that the art teacher from Peoria takes back to her classroom when she says that the conference of the National Committee on Art Education has changed her whole point of view. If these could be described effectively, this report would be much more inspiring; if they could be evaluated, our sense of achievement would be more reassuring.

THE ROLE OF THE ART MUSEUM IN EDUCATION

Does the art museum have a real function in education? Should it deal only with the presentation and interpretation of original works of art? Or should it also concern itself with the large communication media such as motion pictures, radio, and television? Should it offer creative classes in the arts and crafts, or is this solely the province of the public and private school?

These are questions confronting museum educators. Space does not allow a complete answer here, but some of the basic considerations can be explored. The feeling exists that an art museum may merely duplicate the function of the schools by giving art courses; or that it may compete with commercial organizations which produce visual materials, art equipment and toys. The fact is that the need for such materials is so great that if all the organizations involved were to step up production threefold, this would not begin to meet the urgent need of education. And if only those materials which attained a high standard of quality were considered, available materials would be reduced markedly and the lack would be still more pronounced. The experience of the Museum of Modern Art and other museums seriously concerned with education conclusively shows that not only does the museum have a function in education but that this function is unique and necessary. The museum is a valuable source for extending the understanding of the child because it contains original works of art, prints of masterpieces, and models, without which creative experience can be neither profound nor enriching to the individual.

A special function of the educational department in an art museum is to make the art materials used visually appealing and to present them in terms of the perception, needs, and interests of the age levels concerned. The educational department also integrates the various resources of the museum, the expert knowledge of the curators, and the craftsmanship of the designers and technicians with the needs of the child and with the curriculum. Although many efforts have been made by schools or school systems to produce their own visual materials, these efforts have eventually been abandoned in favor of the more important and pressing responsibilities of the teaching program. The school is not equipped nor should it be expected to prepare these materials for itself.

The answer to the question "Should the art museum hold creative classes?" would in many cases depend on the particular museum and on its locality. In regions where sufficient creative opportunity is given to children in the schools, there is no need for the museum to offer creative classes. But such cases are rare. In most situations, a museum must supplement or offer art because schools fail to do so. A more important factor is that the museum can help education by exploring new teaching methods and techniques. As budgets are reduced and art is cur-

tailed in the schools, the need for experimentation, the very life of educational growth, becomes greater. The museum, therefore, is the last remaining area for such experimentation and through this service alone can offer the schools a valuable aid. The art museum has just begun to recognize its role in education. It is still pioneering. With the increased production of visual materials by the commercial firms, many of which are exploiting the child rather than furthering his creative welfare, and with the rise of television as an effective and indelible means of visual communication, the museum, along with other educational institutions, faces a tremendous challenge and responsibility. Unless quality in both aesthetic and educational objectives is maintained, the creative education of our youth is jeopardized.

The Museum of Modern Art. photo Alexandre Georges

STAFF OF THE DEPARTMENT OF EDUCATION

Victor D'Amico, *Director*

Dorothy Knowles, *Assistant to the Director*

Elizabeth Fuller, *Assistant (New York City Public School Program)*

Mrs. Dorothy O'Hara, *Assistant (People's Art Center Program)*

Barbara Ann Douglas, *Secretary to the Director*

Mrs. Bernice B. Cousins, *Secretary for the National Committee on Art Education*

Mrs. Sue Raices, *Clerical Assistant (People's Art Center)*

Mrs. Florence Cooper, *Clerical Assistant (People's Art Center)*

STAFF OF THE PEOPLE'S ART CENTER

Victor D'Amico, *Director*

Instructors:

Alice Adams*
Rex Ashlock†*
Mrs. Jane Cooper Bland†
Mary Ellen Blumenfeld†
Ralph Carpentier*
Abraham L. Chanin*
Mrs. Jean d'Autilia†
Mrs. Tinka Denenberg†
Naomi Freilicoff†
Lilli Gettinger†*
Mrs. Joan Goldberg†
Lorrie Goulet*
June Hildebrand*
Charles Jarm†
Mrs. Margaret Kennard Johnson*
Mrs. Elizabeth Levine†
Mr. Thomas T. Lord†
Bernard Pfriem*
Mrs. Avital Sagalyn†
Mrs. Lucia Salemme†*
Mrs. Ellen Schleicher†
Mrs. Muriel Silberstein†
Mrs. Elizabeth Spiro†*
Donald Stacy*
Sam G. Weiner†*

* Instructor of Adult Classes.
† Instructor of Children's Classes.

Attendants:

Howard Long
Mrs. Marie Green
Mrs. Julia Rohlsen
Walter Munford